# SCHIRMER'S LIBRARY
## OF MUSICAL CLASSICS

Vol. 2117

# Three Romantic Violin Concertos

## Bruch, Mendelssohn, Tchaikovsky

### For Violin and Piano

ISBN 978-1-4950-1042-2

# G. SCHIRMER, Inc.

DISTRIBUTED BY
HAL•LEONARD®
CORPORATION
7777 W. BLUEMOUND RD. P.O. BOX 13819 MILWAUKEE, WI 53213

www.musicsalesclassical.com
www.halleonard.com

# CONTENTS

# Concerto
## for Violin in G minor, Op. 26

### I. Prelude

Edited and fingered by
Henry Schradieck

Max Bruch

2

8

## II. Adagio

14

# III. Finale

# Concerto
## for Violin in E minor, Op. 64

Edited and fingered by
Henry Schradieck

Felix Mendelssohn

38

53

# Concerto
## for Violin in D Major, Op. 35

Edited and fingered by
Philipp Mittell

Pyotr Il'Yich Tchaikovsky

# Canzonetta

94

95

97